A Friend for Einstein

The Smallest Stallion

by Charlie Cantrell and Dr. Rachel Wagner

Little Stallion Publsihing

We wish to express our heartfelt thanks to Stephanie Owens Lurie and her magical team as well as Cheryl Pientka, Jill Grinberg, Mira Pitacin, Sophia Seidner, Mark Wagner, and the rest of Team Einstein for making this book possible. In loving memory of Judy and Larry Smith. A very special thanks goes to all our furry and not-so furry friends in this book.

This book is dedicated with love to Lilly.

Photographs by Charlie Cantrell
Story by Charlie Cantrell and Dr. Rachel Wagner
Author Photograph by Mark Wagner

Far from the loud city streets, just past the rickety-rack of hardworking tractors, and behind the gates of a horse farm, there lived a little foal.

His name was Einstein, and he was the smallest horse ever born. He was a mini miniature horse.

Every morning, after a hearty breakfast of oats, milk, and hay, Einstein would follow his mother out of their stall and into the paddock to explore. He had hooves the size of quarters, and he could walk right under his mother's belly.

Being so low to the ground, Einstein could see things up close, like the speckles on a tiger lily, his favorite flower.

In most ways, though, Einstein was like any other horse.

He loved to gallop and hop,
sniff and trot, and lie
in the warm sun.

One day, while grazing in his pen, Einstein spotted a herd of miniature horses nearby.

They dashed and darted. They zigzagged and sauntered.

Their shiny tails whipped in the wind, and Einstein jumped with excitement, longing to join them.

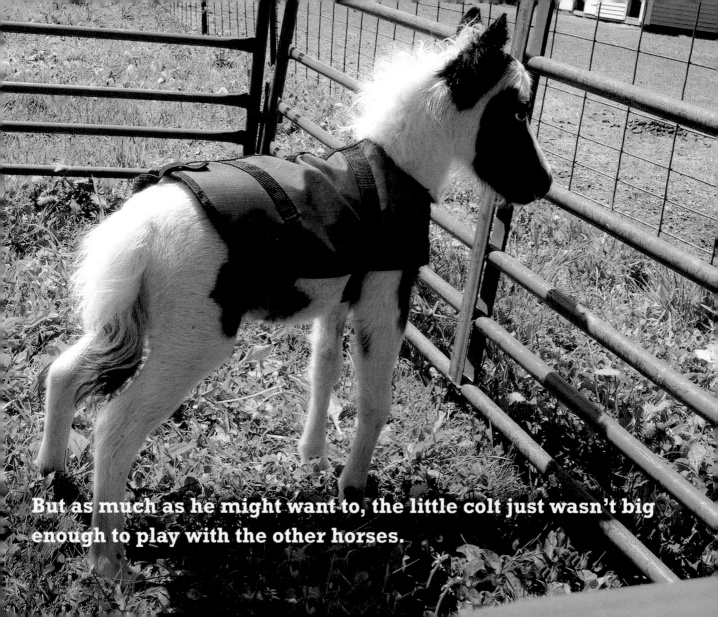

But as much as he might want to, the little colt just wasn't big enough to play with the other horses.

When Einstein went to sleep that night,

he dreamed of the day he could run with the herd.

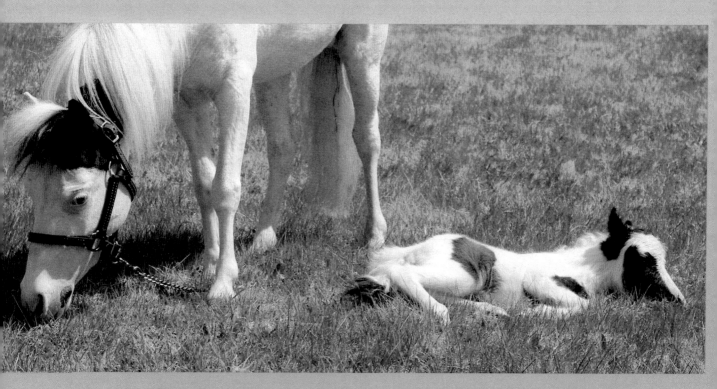

There was no escaping it: Einstein was lonely.

One afternoon, Einstein went in search of a friend. In the field, he came across a pair of kittens. He lowered his head to get a better look, and—ouch!—one of them swatted his muzzle.

They mewed and hissed, scrambled and scurried. Einstein couldn't keep them straight as they wrestled each other. Feeling a little dizzy, he continued on his way. Those crazy cats were definitely not the right playmates for him.

Next, Einstein spotted some ducks by the pond.
Quack-quack-quack-quack-quack!
they said loudly as they waddled off,
clearly not interested
in befriending a horse,
even a little one.

Maybe it was because he didn't know how to swim.

Taking time out for a snack, Einstein noticed something in the grass. It looked like a rock, but then it began to move. All of a sudden, out poked a head! A tortoise! Einstein frisked in front of the gentle reptile, inviting it to play tag. The tortoise followed . . . ever so slowly.

Einstein waited and waited and waited some more, until finally the little stallion couldn't stand it any longer. This friend was *boring*!

A bunny, basking in the golden glow of the afternoon sun, looked more promising.

Eager to play, Einstein nudged it. But the sudden movement frightened the nervous rabbit.

Einstein watched sadly as the bashful bunny hopped away.

Poor Einstein. The animals he'd met were either too silly, too stuck up, too slow, or too shy. Why was it so difficult to find a friend? Maybe little stallions were just meant to be lonesome. He headed for the barn, where at least his mother would be waiting for him.

Back by his pen, Einstein was in for a surprise. An odd-looking creature was poking through the fence. It was a dog with a snub nose, wrinkly eyes, and a head as big as the moon.

She didn't have much of a tail, but what she did have was wiggling.

Her name was Lilly, like the speckled flower in the pasture.

Slowly, carefully, Einstein scooted a little bit closer to investigate. The big dog opened her huge mouth and . . .

SLURPPP!

She gave him a big kiss.

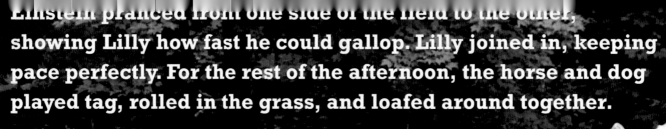

Einstein pranced from one side of the field to the other, showing Lilly how fast he could gallop. Lilly joined in, keeping pace perfectly. For the rest of the afternoon, the horse and dog played tag, rolled in the grass, and loafed around together.

It was as if they had known each other forever.

The little horse with a big heart had finally found his friend.

Authors' Note:

When horse lovers Charlie Cantrell and his wife, Dr. Rachel Wagner, received the news that a tiny horse had just been born to champion miniature horses, they knew they had to meet the mini-miniature foal. Sure enough, it was love at first sight, and Charlie bought the baby as a present for Rachel, an experienced rider and owner of a number of horses

Two weeks after Einstein was born, the Cantrells were shocked to discover a procession of 4,000 visitors, soggy and shivering in the rain, lined up to pay homage to their little horse. Cars were parked all the way to the center of the small New England town, and local police had to shut the roads down a mile from Einstein's barn and turn many more cars away. Some people stood for over an hour just to get a sixty-second glimpse of the fast-asleep baby stallion.

As Charlie and Rachel greeted the half-mile line of fans from all walks of life, they immediately recognized an unmistakable connection among the crowd: Einstein elicited a feeling of pure joy and remarkable gladness in everyone he touched. The good feeling spread as videos of newborn Einstein swept the Internet. Within days the tiny foal was featured in newspapers, magazines, and television programs as far away as Australia.

As much as Einstein's adoring fans wanted more, Charlie and Rachel knew that he needed to live as if he were no different from other horses. They created this book to share their magical little horse with the world.

Made in the USA
Las Vegas, NV
21 December 2020

14360128R00019